Original title:
Vines in My Dreams

Copyright © 2025 Creative Arts Management OÜ
All rights reserved.

Author: Julian Prescott
ISBN HARDBACK: 978-1-80581-871-7
ISBN PAPERBACK: 978-1-80581-398-9
ISBN EBOOK: 978-1-80581-871-7

Blooms Beneath the Starlit Sky

Under stars, the plants confide,
With secrets that they can't hide.
They giggle and sway in the breeze,
Making jokes like expert tease.

The daisies dance, the lilies chuckle,
In the moonlight, they all snuggle.
A petal tickles a sleepy rose,
And off it sneezes—how it goes!

Tangles of Sleep and Slumber

In my dreams, the weeds conspire,
Knots and twists, they never tire.
A thistle winks, a dandelion grins,
   As I tumble into their spins.

Sleepy buds play hide and seek,
Whispering pranks with silly tweaks.
They pull my toes, they poke my nose,
   In this wild dream, anything goes!

The Garden of Faded Echoes

In shadows where the laughter fades,
The flowers spin in light cascades.
They whisper tales of days gone by,
With every petal, a chuckle sighs.

A sunflower wears a quirky hat,
While bees complain of a spat.
"Buzz off!" one flower vainly shouts,
As others join in raucous clouts!

Echoes of a Twisted Hush

In silence deep, the blooms conspire,
To juggle dreams, a floral choir.
With a nudge, the tulips start,
A riot of giggles, a bursting heart.

The ferns make faces, the roses tease,
While daisies fall into fits of wheeze.
The garden laughs, oh what a show!
As night descends, the fun won't slow!

The Secret Life of Twining Stems

In the garden, whispers creep,
Where shy creepers play and leap.
They twist and twirl with giggly flair,
Like sneaky dancers caught in air.

A chicken clucks, it joins the fun,
As tangled stems absorb the sun.
Each leaf a hat, each bud a crown,
They carnival it up, no chance to frown!

Intricate Labyrinths of the Mind

In my thoughts, they weave and spin,
Like mazes where a cat might grin.
I chase a thought, it runs away,
A leafy prankster in my day!

Twisting pathways, oh so sly,
Leading me to wonder why.
At every turn, a new surprise,
A hedgehog wearing fancy ties!

Dancing Among the Shrubs

The bushes sway, a lively crew,
With frolicsome leaves in a merry hue.
They shimmy, shake, and pull a pose,
In the style of friends, they strike a rose.

A squirrel joins, he's got some moves,
With pitter-patter, he grooves and grooves.
The petals chuckle, the grass joins in,
As nature hosts a cheerful din!

Whispers That Tangle in the Breeze

The whispers float on breezy flights,
Like giggling fairies, oh what sights!
They twist and twirl, oh what a tease,
    Sending secrets through the trees.

I hear them laugh, they jest and play,
    Tickling branches along the way.
    A polka-dotted snail appears,
He's dressed for joy, to spread some cheers!

Embracing the Wilderness of Thought

In the wilds of my mind, thoughts twist and twine,
Like slippery snakes at a funky design.
They giggle and wiggle, just trying to play,
Trying to lead my poor brain astray.

In a jungle of ideas, I stumble and slip,
Chasing these whispers, I hop, skip, and trip.
A parade of confusion, a cartoonish chase,
I grin at the madness, it's all part of the race.

Thoughts jump like frogs, with a flippity-flop,
Each leap a new riddle, each bounce a new bop.
They chuckle and tease, in a tumble of fun,
While I navigate chaos under the sun.

So here in this forest, I'll dance with delight,
Embracing the chaos, from morning to night.
With laughter and whimsy, I'll carry the load,
In the wilderness twist, I've found my abode.

The Dance of Tendrils and Stars

Beneath twinkling skies, their lengths twist and twirl,
   They tickle the cosmos, like boy meets girl.
With a prance and a bounce, they reach for the sun,
   Each tendril a giggle, oh what fun has begun!

   They leap through the night, in a wobbly spin,
   Wrapping around memories, in a playful grin.
   Like puppets on strings in a whimsical play,
   They frolic and twist 'til the break of the day.

   With a chuckle and toss, they swing into air,
     Giggling and dancing, sans a single care.
   They flirt with the moon, in a giggly embrace,
     Creating a ruckus in this starry space.

   As laughter erupts from the ground up to sky,
   The tendrils rejoice, and I can't help but sigh.
     For in this circus, I find pure delight,
In the dance of the stars, the world feels just right.

Heartstrings Tied to Nature's Bow

In the garden where green things roam,
I found a snake wearing a tiny comb.
It giggled and danced, did a silly twist,
Wearing a hat on its head—oh, the bliss!

A turtle in shades sipped tea on a stone,
Claiming he'd just won a race all alone.
With a wink and a grin, he invited me too,
But I laughed so hard, I just couldn't get through.

The Lure of Lush Enigmas

The broccoli trees began to sway,
I asked them to stop, but they wouldn't obey.
They hummed little tunes in a vibrant green,
Dancing around like they're part of a scene.

A pepper in a tux led a leafy parade,
While carrots in costumes played charades.
I clapped and I laughed, it was quite the plot,
Never knew veggies could throw such a hot shot!

In the Shadow of Ancient Green

Beneath the canopy of leafy dread,
A squirrel in glasses read tales of the dead.
With a chuckle and snort, he turned page after page,
Claiming the forest was quite the fun stage!

Mushrooms in bow ties danced under the light,
Jiving and jiving, oh what a sight!
A fungi conga line made me jump and cheer,
Who knew the woods held such laughter and cheer?

Tidal Waves of Tangled Dreams

In a stream of thought, a fish wore a tie,
He fancied himself quite the suave little guy.
With splashes and flares, he swam through my mind,
Bragging about the treasures he managed to find.

A crab in a crown sang a tune with flair,
Dancing with mermaids who tossed in the air.
Together they giggled, creating a splash,
In dreams full of antics, oh what a bash!

Lurking Beneath the Canopy

Green things creeping, giggling high,
I swear they're planning, oh my my!
They tickle my toes, sneak hugs from behind,
A leafy parade, so bizarrely aligned.

Rambunctious roots play tag with the breeze,
Dancing round puddles like they own the trees!
A mischievous wave in the thick of night,
They whisper my secrets, it's quite a sight!

The Jardin of Forgotten Tales

Once a tale lost in roots so deep,
Where chortles and chuckles awaken from sleep.
A gnome with a shovel, a hat made of cheese,
Digs up the past with rather fine ease.

The daisies all gossip, the roses all sigh,
While carrots debate if they're shy or spry!
In this garden, where nonsense takes flight,
Every bloom tells a joke, oh what a delight!

Tendrils of Hope and Desire

A twist and a twirl, the sprout starts to sing,
Hoping for sunshine, a colorful fling.
They dream of a party with petals and leaves,
Where even the cabbage can shake its wee knees.

With lettuce romancing the bold broccoli,
They dance in the sunlight, oh what a spree!
Each tendril a storyteller, dripping with cheer,
As they conspire to sprinkle joy far and near.

The Enchanted Underbrush

In the tangle of ferns, a party breaks out,
With feisty brown squirrels, who happily shout.
A toad tap dances, while crickets provide,
The music of madness, on this wild ride.

The mushrooms are laughing, they're plotting a game,
While butterflies whisper secrets, oh what a claim!
As shadows grow longer, the mischief ignites,
They waltz through the night, under twinkling lights.

Roots that Bind the Heart

In the garden where giggles grow,
A tomato winks and says hello.
The cucumber dances, a funny sight,
While carrots make puns in the fading light.

With potatoes plotting a birthday surprise,
Chard wears a hat made of butterfly ties.
A radish juggles with its leafy flair,
As beans croon softly, their joy we share.

Gentle Spirals of Afternoon Mist

The sun gives a wink and the leaves all spin,
While playful breezes join in the din.
A daffodil twirls in its golden gown,
And daisies debate who will wear the crown.

Clouds drift like marshmallows in a cozy sky,
As a squirrel brings doughnuts, oh me, oh my!
The sweet scent of laughter fills the warm air,
With every step, we're lost in this flair.

Nurtured by Nature's Whimsy

A bumblebee buzzes in search of a treat,
While mushrooms organize a tap dance meet.
In the shade of the oak, a picnic's unfurled,
Where ants are the waiters in this funny world.

The breeze whispers secrets of frolic and fun,
As petals play tag in the warm glowing sun.
Grasshoppers chirp out a jazz-filled refrain,
Turning the meadow to a quirky domain.

Ethereal Hotel of the Overgrown

The ivy checks in with a snicker and grin,
While ferns fold their arms and attempt to win.
A sunflower receptionist, bright and stout,
Takes reservations from clouds wandering about.

Slumbering daisies sleep on plush green beds,
While crickets serve cocktails and weave silly threads.
In this leafy lodge, laughter's the key,
Where nature's shenanigans run wild and free.

Lush Fantasies Unfurled

In a garden where ferns can conspire,
A gnome just lit a tiny bonfire.
The daisies gossip, oh what a sight,
While mushrooms giggle with pure delight.

A snail wears shades, so chic and cool,
While ants are dancing, breaking the rule.
The daisies dance, in skirts of bright haze,
In this wild party of leafy malaise.

The Garden of Unspoken Wishes

A pumpkin rides a silver kite,
While turtles race, yet take their flight.
The flowers whisper their hidden dreams,
As petals twirl like chocolate streams.

In this blissful realm of wacky blooms,
Where sugar plums hum and shadow looms.
The rainbows chat, with colors so bold,
Sprinkling laughter like whispers of gold.

Where Shadows Creep and Climb

A shadow slipped, wearing mismatched socks,
While squirrels debate the trickiest locks.
The morning glories are wearing frowns,
As wind swirls past like clownish gowns.

In every nook, a riddle does sparkle,
While loopy branches start to markle.
The sun has taken a silly dive,
Chasing giggles where nonsense thrives.

Entwined in a Celestial Dance

Stars are twirling with giggles and fuss,
While galaxies ride the subway bus.
Comets jest with tails made of cheese,
Descending softly in moonlit breeze.

Planets wear hats, quite plump and round,
With gravity game of silly abound.
As laughter echoes through cosmic lanes,
The universe shakes with joyful refrains.

Secrets Beneath the Blossoming Sky

In the garden where the daisies dance,
A squirrel wearing sunglasses took a chance.
He tried to sip from a flowered cup,
But the nectar made him hiccup and jump.

The bees were buzzing, holding a debate,
About the best flower to decorate.
One thought it was the grand old rose,
While another insisted it's the buttercup's nose.

The butterflies laughed in a colorful spree,
As the bumblebee played the bumblebee spree.
"Join us for tea!" they all began to chime,
While the rabbit grinned, looking for a rhyme.

With a wink and a nudge, they cheered and swayed,
Spilling secrets like confetti, they played.
Under the blossoming canopy's might,
Not a single worry was in sight.

An Odyssey Through Luxuriant Trails

Through winding trails where the daisies peek,
A frog in a bowtie began to speak.
He claimed he was a prince on a day-off spree,
Seeking the 'Magic Pond' to set him free.

The turtles wore hats, quite suave and neat,
While the squirrels coordinated a dance beat.
Every branch played host to a squeaky choir,
Serenading the sun as it climbed higher.

Along the path, a hedgehog held a sign,
"Please don't touch, I'm saving this for a rhyme!"
With giggles and chuckles, they pranced and played,
On this muddy, vibrant parade they made.

As dusk approached with a sparkling hue,
A firefly asked, "What's new with you?"
The creatures all chuckled, "We're just feeling grand,
On this silly, whimsical, leafy land!"

A Medley of Shadows and Flourish

Among the shadows where the flowers twirl,
A dancing snail got caught in a whirl.
He slipped on a petal and landed quite funny,
Saying, "Is this what they call honeysuckle honey?"

A cat in a hat joined in with delight,
Juggling acorns, trying to take flight.
"Look at me, I'm a circus star!"
While the crickets played their goofiest guitar.

The shadows threw parties while the moon tickled beams,
And the frogs croaked out their wildest dreams.
"Let's have a feast!" yelled a cheeky mouse,
As they feasted on crumbs from the neighboring house.

With laughter and joy spinning round in the air,
They celebrated spring with a silly flair.
In the medley of shadows, where stories entwine,
Whimsy is the thread that makes it divine.

Explorations in a Wild Heart

In a thicket where the wildflowers grow,
A raccoon told tales of a funny show.
He wore a bow and tapped a coconut drum,
Creating a beat that made all hearts hum.

A parrot perched high, squawking with glee,
"I'm the star of this jungle, just wait and see!"
His jokes flew like arrows, sharp and bright,
While the monkeys swung by, giggling in flight.

A hedgehog held court with a sparkling stare,
Claiming the title of the brave teddy bear.
"You think you can leap? I'll tell you the way,
With puns and high-fives, we'll dance till the day!"

So in this wild heart of laughter and play,
Every creature found a reason to sway.
With poppy seed dreams and silliness stark,
They wrote their own saga, leaving a mark.

Whispers of Green Shadows

In the garden, secrets dance,
Twisting, turning, in a trance.
A leafy laugh, a playful shout,
What are these greens laughing about?

They tickle toes, they snag at shoes,
A leafy army, winning news.
Their leafy fingers, a gentle tease,
Trying to get me, oh, with ease!

A creeping laugh, I twist and shout,
"Hey, who's the joker? Let me out!"
But plants just giggle, whirly, spry,
As I dodge the dandelions flying by!

Glimmers of green, they hold their ground,
In this silly battle, I'm spellbound.
With every step, they sway and prance,
In this wacky, wild, garden dance!

Twining Tendrils of Hope

They twist and twirl, in a game so grand,
Pretending they're an unplanned band.
With laughter wrapped around each leaf,
Swaying softly, what a cheeky thief!

They pull my shoes, they steal my hat,
I shout, "Now, that's where laughter's at!"
With every tiptoe, they snicker and tease,
A ticklish tango, oh, suddenly it frees!

Banana peels slick on the ground,
With each funny slip, falling down!
The tendrils giggle as I take flight,
In this wacky show of pure delight!

In this green realm, such joy does bloom,
With every twist, I face my doom.
Yet with their laughter surrounding me,
In this humorous play, I'm finally free!

Echoes of Twisted Growth

In the thicket, the laughter grows,
Tap dancing roots and silly toes.
Chasing shadows that play and prance,
In this leafy world, I join the dance!

With tendrils wrapping round my feet,
Each step's a game, oh, what a feat!
They whisper jokes in rustling ways,
In this wild green, we'll spend our days!

Giggles echo through leafy halls,
As nature's punchline breaks my falls.
Their winks are tricksters, light as air,
I stumble, I tumble, without a care!

With every chuckle, the laughter spreads,
Dancing the night with leafy heads.
In tangled chaos, we find our fun,
In echoes of green, joy has begun!

Night's Embrace of Nature

Under moonlight, shadows creep,
Nature's comedy makes me peep.
With every rustle, a quickened beat,
Those silly greens can't be discreet!

Laughter lingers in the night,
As plants throw parties, what a sight!
They tango wildly, roots take flight,
In this leafy wild, all feels right!

A quick retreat from clumsy feet,
Dodging blooms that dance and greet.
Their whispers tickle, a merry bunch,
In this dark theater, I take the plunge!

With giggles stitched through midnight air,
Nature's jesters dance without a care.
In the embrace of the starry schemes,
I find my joy in their funny dreams!

The Tendril's Soft Caress

In the garden, plants conspire,
Tangled whispers, never tire.
A cucumber wears a tiny hat,
Says, "Look at me, I'm quite the brat!"

A sprout that dances on a breeze,
Tickles the daisies with such ease.
Laughter ripples through the green,
It's the funniest sight I've seen!

A strawberry jokes, 'I'm the best treat!'
But everyone knows it can't take heat.
The carrots giggle underground,
Making puns that bounce around.

When moonlight shines, they throw a bash,
With evil weeds that talk too brash.
In this party of leafy cheer,
I can't help but stay right here!

Dreams Cascading Downward

I dream of plants in funny hats,
Dancing 'round with giggling cats.
A pumpkin rolls and cracks a joke,
Even the scarecrow starts to poke!

Raindrops chuckle as they fall,
A waltz of laughter, nature's call.
The sunbeams snicker from the sky,
While tiny bugs all buzz and fly.

Slipping through a leafy slide,
A butterfly takes quite the ride.
It lands on broccoli, what a sight,
"Mmmm, smells like dinner, quite all right!"

In dreams so wild, we laugh till dawn,
With every leaf a whimsical yawn.
As morning breaks, we sigh and say,
"Let's live another goofy day!"

Gardens Beyond the Veil

In gardens veiled from human eyes,
Plants plot mischief, oh what a surprise!
A sunflower grins with sunflower seeds,
While daisies giggle at their silly deeds.

The beans are dreaming of sky-high stakes,
Climbing fences, causing breaks.
"They can't catch us," they boast with glee,
As butterflies watch, sipping their tea.

Potatoes roll, but wait—what's that?
A rogue tomato in a spat!
"Is this a garden or circus ground?
We should start a show, we're quite renowned!"

So if you wander through the green,
Listen closely for the unseen.
For in that laughter, joy will swell,
In gardens hidden, tales they tell!

Enchanted Roots Beneath the Moon

Beneath the moon, roots start to scheme,
With whispers soft, like a wild dream.
A mushroom pulls a prank on the soil,
Making earthworms jiggle and coil.

A nightly dance, the crickets cheer,
As cabbages court their partner near.
"We'll have a ball," the lettuce sways,
While glowing fireflies light the ways.

"Let's tell jokes!" the garlic cries,
And lemon balm rolls around and sighs.
"Your punchlines stink, they need some zest!"
But still, they chuckle, never stressed.

As twilight fades, they plot once more,
Adventurous tales from roots to floor.
Their laughter lingers in night's embrace,
With funny dreams, this lively space!

Lattice of Forgotten Sorrows

In a garden, I took a stroll,
Tripping over my own shoe sole.
Tangled tales and laughter blend,
As I chase my thoughts, they lend.

A gnome is laughing, what a sight,
His hat is crooked, quite a plight.
Whispers of old, in leafy jest,
Tell me, who wears the funniest vest?

Puns grow wild along the path,
A tree just told a math class laugh!
I ponder deep in leafy green,
Is this garden or unseen scene?

At twilight's curtain, I declare,
These antics sprout, fresh as a pear.
With every step, the jokes unfold,
In this lattice, my whims are bold.

Nature's Silent Serenade

Beneath the shade, I hear a tune,
A frog's croak, a bouncing balloon.
Bees are buzzing in a choir,
Tickling flowers, never tire.

Leaves sing softly, oh so grand,
As I hum with nature's band.
The sky's a canvas, blue and bright,
But my hat just took off in flight!

Squirrels are plotting, mischief high,
Building castles up in the sky.
Nature giggles, I crack a grin,
In this realm, I've found my kin.

Whispers of joy dance in the breeze,
With stumbles and trips, I'm at ease.
In the silence, a symphony beams,
As I laugh loud, ye gods, it seems!

Echoes Beneath the Overgrowth

Hidden giggles in tangled twine,
A lost sock? It must be mine!
Shadows play, with cheeky flair,
As beetles form a marching square.

Rustling leaves, a playful tease,
Mockingbirds mimic my sneeze!
While I ponder the oddest jest,
A snail shows me just how to rest.

Echoes bounce from twigs so sly,
As butterflies laugh and flutter by.
Who knew woods held such fun games,
Chasing spirits, no two the same?

In the thicket where whispers grow,
Epic tales of laughter flow.
In a chase for the absurd, I find,
Joy is lurking, ever so kind!

A World Woven in Green

In a patchwork land of vibrant hues,
Where daisies wear the silliest shoes.
Chasing feathers in the wind,
Each stumble leaves a laugh distilled.

Mossy stones are throwing shade,
As rabbits hop in jingled parade.
This place is wild, with whimsy bright,
Even the moon is giggling tonight!

Frolicsome figs and nuts to crack,
In this banquet, there's no lack.
Wild laughter twirls among the leaves,
As I dance with vines that tease and weave.

Among the greens, joy's contagious,
Every tickle feels outrageous.
In this world wrapped tight in glee,
I chuckle softly, wild and free!

Boundless Greenery Awaits

In a jungle made of spaghetti,
Lions dance in a tutu, so petty.
Monkeys juggling ripe bananas,
While parrots sing in velvet pajamas.

Tangled webs of licorice swirls,
Hippos twirl in their polka-dot pearls.
The trees wear hats of fluffy marshmallows,
As squirrels strut in sparkling bellows.

The Secret Language of Leaves

Whispering secrets after the rain,
Leaves gossip about the sun's stain.
A maple winked at a curious oak,
While birches giggled at a sly folk.

They talk of beetles with shiny backs,
And caterpillars playing tic-tac-tacks.
One leaf sneezed, it made a great sound,
As others laughed, twirling around.

Threads of Imagination

In the garden where dreams are spun,
Rabbits race; they think it's fun.
Daisies dance to a polka beat,
While gnomes tap their tiny feet.

Crickets wear bow ties, oh so neat,
Under mushrooms, they find a seat.
Fireflies flash like disco lights,
Creating parties on starry nights.

Beneath a Canopy of Stars

Stars hang like piñatas on high,
As raccoons plot their dessert supply.
Beneath the canopy, laughter flows,
With giggling shadows and silly toes.

A turtle in slippers takes a stroll,
While owls hoot softly, a nighttime goal.
Fireflies join in a glow-tastic dance,
As crickets serenade in a playful trance.

Serenity in Twisted Growth

In a garden where giggles entwine,
Snakes of green dance, oh how they twine.
They tickle the toes of sleepy old men,
Who wake up in laughter, then sleep again.

Whispers of lettuce joke with the breeze,
While carrots wear hats and invite you to tease.
A cabbage serenades a lost bumblebee,
In this wacky patch, all's quirky and free.

Forget the mundane, enjoy the odd sights,
As tomatoes play chess under starlit nights.
With every twist, the world spins so bright,
Let's toast with our radish, a delightful bite!

So come take a stroll in this whimsical place,
Where laughter grows wild and time has no pace.
Each plant tells a story of giggles and cheer,
In this garden of chaos, there's nothing to fear.

Forest of Insomnolent Dreams

In a forest where snores turn to songs,
Trees wear pajamas, not dresses, nor throngs.
Bear tries to dance but trips on his paws,
As raccoons build forts with their whimsical claws.

Owls in spectacles read under the moon,
While fireflies waltz to a soft, sleepy tune.
A skunk learns ballet, though he stinks up the show,
And turtles line up, cheering 'Go, slowpoke, go!'

The night air is thick with giggly delight,
As spiders spin webs that shine oh-so-bright.
A dog dressed as Santa collects all the cheer,
While dreams prance around, whispering near.

Join the parade of this slumbering land,
Where every odd creature lends a helping hand.
They laugh at the sun as it starts to arise,
In this woodland of whimsy, joy never dies.

The Delicate Path of Growth

Along a path where chuckles unfold,
Flowers wear sneakers, oh so bold.
A daisy in shades says, 'Life's pure delight!'
While a rose tells a joke that's just out of sight.

Lilies on scooters zoom with glee,
While mushrooms argue on how to be free.
A snail wins a race, slow but so wise,
Leaving all bunnies in awe of his size.

The sun winks at daisies, as they dance in a line,
While clouds rain confetti, how perfectly fine!
Every petal's a giggle, each leaf's a grin,
On this path of delight, where fun's bound to win!

So skip with the blooms down this road of delight,
With laughter and joy, everything feels right.
For growth isn't solemn, it's a colorful spree,
And in this merry garden, we're all wild and free!

Ethereal Sprouts of Yearning

In a realm where giggles take flight,
Sprouts dream of laughs, in colors so bright.
A sprightly onion peeks out with a grin,
As flowers create symphonies, where to begin?

Cucumbers play tag with the raindrops above,
While zucchini offers hugs, warm as a glove.
Each leaf holds a secret, a giggly cheer,
As the wind tells a tale, lending all an ear.

Tomatoes in bowties invite you for tea,
While peas do a jig, as happy as can be.
Pumpkins roll by, with a fit of good cheer,
In this garden of mirth, all worries disappear.

So come join the frolic, dance under the sun,
In this magical garden, where laughter is fun.
Each sprout sings a song, each vine has a tale,
Here, joy springs eternal, and laughter prevails.

Embrace of the Verdant Spirits

In a garden of giggles, they sway,
Dancing like socks on laundry day.
With twists and turns, they try to hide,
From the tickles of bugs that glide.

A sprout with a sneeze lets out a shout,
While a leafy fellow has no doubts.
They whisper secrets to the air,
While others just play tag, unaware.

In a pot, one sprout tells a joke,
All the other plants giggle, then poke.
The sun's bright rays are their disco light,
As they sway and bounce, what a silly sight!

So join the fun in this leafy world,
Where laughs and curls are twirled and whirled.
In the arms of emerald cheer they bend,
Silly spirits, always ready to send.

Roots of Yearning in the Dark

Buried deep in soil's embrace,
The roots are plotting with little grace.
They twist and poke in whispers low,
Dreaming of the sunshine's glow.

One root says, 'Let's reach for the sky!'
Another snickers, 'But how, oh my?'
They wiggle and jiggle, what a sight,
In the dark where they must take flight.

A moonlit frolic, an underground race,
They giggle and trip, oh what a chase!
With nibbled leaves as their makeshift hats,
They party at night, those silly brats!

So if you wander in silent night's park,
You may hear the fun beneath the dark.
Roots may yearn, but oh how they play,
In a soil-bound jig, celebrating the day!

The Serpent's Lullaby

In a curl of green, a serpent dreams,
With giggles that bubble like soft ice creams.
He sings to the flowers, a tune so sweet,
While roses tumble, swept off their feet.

Every note tickles the petals bright,
And they sway and whirl, quite a silly sight.
Others join in, a waltz in the grass,
As the silly serpent plays with sass.

Around him the daisies twist and shout,
"Is that a lullaby or a funny bout?"
With laughter like rain, they dance in delight,
Under the watch of the blushing night.

A funky serenade in nature's core,
Where all are invited for a fun encore.
So come join the party wherever it lies,
In the melody spun by the serpent's sighs!

Nature's Cascading Dreams

In a waterfall made of sprightly beams,
The rocks join in with nature's schemes.
They slip and slide in a giggle spree,
Water gushing with carefree glee.

Frogs leap in rhythm, all to the beat,
Each splash echoing like a dance in the heat.
A turtle triplets in a very slow groove,
While the trees take a bow, with a wobbly move.

The sunlight sparkles, a playful dance,
With shadows that prance in a comical glance.
As the breeze whispers jokes to the brook,
Nature smiles wide, let's take a look!

So gather your laughter, let's make a mess,
In cascading dreams, feel the happiness.
With nature as joker, so wild and free,
Join this funny romp, come laugh with me!

The Endless Spiral of the Soul

In the garden of my mind, I weave,
Twisting thoughts like a mischief-making reprieve.
They dance like bees around my head,
Chasing shadows of things I never said.

With every turn, a new idea springs,
Like rubber bands that snap with silly flings.
They loop and coil, then take a dive,
What wacky wonders, in dreams, arrive!

I see them laughing, these twirling stains,
Creating comedies from my tangled brains.
A parade of thoughts that wiggle and shout,
Who knew my mind was a circus, no doubt?

So let them twine, let them spin, let them play,
These oddball fancies brighten my day.
In the spiral, I find joy and jest,
In the labyrinth of thoughts, I am truly blessed.

Between Leaves of Memory and Light

In a forest where laughter mingles with bliss,
Leafy whispers tell tales of what we miss.
Each leaf a secret, rustling delight,
Tickling my dreams in the soft moonlight.

A squirrel in a suit, with a briefcase of nuts,
Grins wide as he skips, oh what silly cuts!
He juggles my memories, drops one or two,
With a wink of his eye, he sneaks in a chew.

Beneath shining stars, the branches entwine,
As fireflies giggle, there's joy to define.
A maze of memories, both funny and bright,
In the glow of this night, everything feels right.

So let the leaves fall, let the laughter grow,
In the simplicity, there's so much to know.
The cuddly chaos of dreams takes flight,
In a mosaic of colors, I dance through the night.

The Subtle Art of Growth in Slumber

In my sleep garden where giggles bloom,
I find tiny tomatoes that hop in a room.
They tumble and roll, boisterous little things,
Wearing bright hats while they dance and sing.

With a wink from a cucumber, oh so sly,
He whispers of dreams that reach to the sky.
We build castles with pillows and giggle with glee,
As the moon sends us whispers of wild jubilee.

Each night is a banquet of whimsical fare,
A feast of oddities, who could compare?
With all this growth in the land of my rest,
I'm a dreamer, a grower, enchantingly blessed.

So let slumber take me where silliness reigns,
In fields of delight, there are no mundane chains.
In the tapestry woven of dreams without strife,
I cultivate laughter, the essence of life!

Ties That Bind

With a twirl and a leap, I chase my own tail,
In a spaghetti of thoughts, I cannot fail.
They knot and entwine, a tangle so grand,
In this silly mosaic, I simply must stand.

A shoelace of laughter, a ribbon of cheer,
Binds my essence, keeps me near.
With friends made of daisies and giggles so sweet,
We dance in a circle, with joy at our feet.

Each twist and each turn in this vibrant play,
Reminds me of moments that lead me astray.
We sever the ties that we once found mundane,
To build up the laughter, that's our merry gain.

For in the chaos, I find my own kind,
Ties that are perfect, uniquely designed.
With smiles as our anchors, we're never confined,
In the garden of friendship, true joy is defined.

Dreams That Release

In the parlor of my thoughts, a balloon takes flight,
Filled with giggles, it pops in delight.
Releasing the dreams that were stored all along,
They swirl in the air, like a whimsical song.

A tap dance on clouds, a waltz with the sun,
Nonsense reigns where the laughter has run.
Each thought like a bubble, floating away,
Exploding with joy—what a marvelous play!

I chase shooting stars that giggle and tease,
Lucky enough to hug the playful breeze.
In the chaos of dreams, a carnival spins,
Life's little hiccups turn into silly wins.

So catch those wild dreams, let the laughter increase,
In a world full of whimsy, I find my release.
With every silly moment, I rise and I shine,
In the dreams that connect us, both yours and mine.

Boundless Trails of the Mind

Through tangled thoughts I tumble down,
Chasing shadows that wear a crown.
A squirrel whispers with a cheeky grin,
Who knew the waltz would begin within?

In puddles of dreams where puddles splash,
With giggles and bubbles, oh what a clash!
I sway with bubbles, they pop and flee,
Is this a dance? Come join with me!

Around corners, I find a hat,
A wise old frog sits, how about that?
He croaks a tune, a jolly bard,
We laugh 'til we drop, oh, it ain't hard!

With a wink at the stars that wiggle above,
I trip on clouds, it's all a big love.
So if you join this rollicking spree,
We'll paint the world with glee, just you and me!

Secrets in the Garden's Heart

In a plot thick with tales of jest,
A gnome confesses, he must confess!
He snickers at ants, plotting their course,
While daisies gossip with vivid remorse.

A ladybug swoops, all decked in red,
With tales of pollen as if it were bread.
I roll on the grass, a soft cozy nest,
And lose all my worries, that silly quest.

The sun winks down, a cheeky old chap,
As fruits in the trees begin their nap.
With playful kisses rustling through,
The garden's secrets sing just for you!

Who knew that laughter blooms from each seed?
Amongst the green leaves, no one takes heed.
So pull up a chair, don't be shy, my friend,
In this garden of dreams, the laughter won't end!

The Pulse of Life Entwined

With vines that giggle, tickle and sway,
They braid my thoughts in a jolly ballet.
A parrot squawks in a vibrant hue,
"Let's dance together, it's good for you!"

Bouncing on branches, a squirrel's parade,
In acorn hats, what a silly charade!
With each hop and leap, a cheer they drum,
"Join the party!" they laugh, "Oh, here we come!"

The breeze plays a tune, a whimsical tune,
While fireflies twinkle like stars in June.
We stumble through shadows, breathless with mirth,
In the garden of life, we find our worth.

With every twist, a chuckle appears,
In the dance of existence, we shed all our fears.
So let's prance on this path, all tangled and sweet,
Life's pulse carries laughter, a playful heartbeat!

Emerald Murmurs of the Night

In the hush of night, hear a soft giggle,
The moon plays tricks and starts to wiggle.
With shadows that dance, quite out of tune,
They trip over stars, oh what a boon!

A raccoon with flair takes center stage,
Reciting old tales of a wise old sage.
With a berry hat perched on his head,
He spins yarns of cheese, so delightfully spread.

And in the corners, secrets do creep,
As owls snap selfies, oh what a heap!
The grasses whisper sweet lullabies,
While fireflies twirl, a dance in the skies.

So take off your shoes, and wiggle your toes,
The night is alive with laughter that flows.
In this forest of frolic, let joy take flight,
With emerald murmurs to guide us tonight!

Serene Whispers from the Earth

In the twilight, plants conspire,
Cotton candy dreams on wire.
Silly thoughts they tend to spin,
Talking plants, let the fun begin!

Wiggling roots and dancing leaves,
Tripping on what twilight weaves.
Whispered jokes from soil so deep,
Giggles sprout where shadows creep.

Carrots dress in evening gowns,
Cucumbers wear the finest crowns.
Every seed throws quite a bash,
Hiding friends in tangled trash!

So when you stroll through grassy trails,
Listen close to nature's tales.
Healing laughs and leafy cheer,
Earth's a comedian, never fear!

The Grasp of Lush Illusions

In a garden where hijinks bloom,
Daisies wear their best costume.
Marigolds play peek-a-boo,
While daisies yell out, "Boo to you!"

Wacky weeds with whims to share,
Chasing cats who're unaware.
Each sunflower a stand-up star,
Joking 'bout the moon and tar!

Lettuce heads exchange some seeds,
Trading puns in leafy creeds.
And every sprout, with laughter peaks,
Hoots and hollers, true leaf sheiks!

So if you think the garden's bland,
Look for giggles in the land.
With every bloom a story told,
Nature's humor never gets old!

Nightfall's Silken Intricacies

When night descends with quirky flair,
Spiders weave tales in midair.
Creepy crawlers join the dance,
Wobbling under moon's soft glance.

The toads croak out a jolly tune,
While fireflies flash in pirate's swoon.
Mice play tag with shadows so bold,
Whispers of magic in the cold.

Each petal glows in silken thought,
As crickets spin tales truly caught.
In velvet whispers, night birds call,
Giggling softly through it all.

So wander forth where moonbeams play,
In dreamworlds where the silly stay.
Nighttime's laughter fills the air,
Beneath the stars without a care!

Delicate Fantasies in Green

Amidst the greens, a funny tale,
Frogs wear hats and leaves sail.
Puppy paws make muddy art,
Nature giggles from the start.

The daisies twist and shout with glee,
As bumblebees sip their sweet tea.
With every sprout a wild prank,
Peeking gnomes in the garden bank!

Chasing shadows, butterflies whirl,
Laughter dances, petals unfurl.
Each sprig a jester in disguise,
Winking with mischievous eyes.

So revel in this dreamlike shade,
Where playful mirth is freely laid.
In every leaf, a chuckle sings,
As playful joy around us flings!

The Hush of Foliage and Dream

In a garden where whispers play,
Foliage plots in a cheeky way.
Leaves gossip, sharing juicy news,
About the antics of the morning dews.

A snail races down a leafy hill,
Claims he's the fastest, what a thrill!
But when a worm outslips his pace,
Oh, how he sulks with a slow-motion face.

Butterflies toss a wild tea party,
Sipping nectar, feeling so hearty.
A bumblebee crashes, spills the beans,
Claims he's the king of these green scenes.

At dusk, the foliage starts to dance,
Grasses jiggle in a evening trance.
In this world where fun never ceases,
Nature laughs as joy increases.

Spiraling Thoughts of the Wilderness

In a forest where the trees conspire,
Squirrels plot like they're on fire.
Branches twist in comical delight,
Wrapping up sounds of pure bite.

A raccoon sings out of tune,
With a late-night snack by the light of the moon.
He thinks he's the star of the woodland show,
But the owls just hoot, 'Oh, what a blow!'

Mushrooms giggle, tickled by dew,
Fungi gather for a laugh or two.
Nature's absurdity brings such cheer,
A downtown squirrel knows no fear.

As shadows stretch and laughter grows,
The wildest thoughts everyone knows:
In spirals of mirth, our dreams expand,
Nature's chuckle, wide and grand.

The Timeless Dance of Green

In emerald fields where the clovers prance,
Daisies wear hats, join in the dance.
The wind waltzes with joyful flair,
Rustling secrets of fresh air.

Caterpillars groove on a leafy floor,
Practicing moves for the butterfly tour.
They spin and twirl, what a grand sight,
Dreaming of wings, oh what a flight!

A cricket chirps a silly tune,
Telling the flowers they'll be on soon.
Bees join in with a buzzing choir,
Hymns of sweetness, lifting us higher.

As night falls, the moon takes a bow,
Grasshoppers jump, "You should join us now!"
The timeless dance of green brings glee,
In a world where laughter roams free.

A Symphony of Leaf and Twilight

Twilight settles like a cozy quilt,
As leaves assemble with cunningly built.
The orchestra starts with a rustling sound,
Nature's concert, we're all spellbound.

The frogs croak a bass line quite bold,
While crickets add chirps, shiny and gold.
A firefly twinkles, lighting the scene,
With flickers of rhythm, oh so keen!

Branches sway to the musical breeze,
Whispering secrets among the trees.
A squirrel beats drums on a hollow log,
While raccoons dance under the night fog.

In this symphony, laughter's the key,
Where the whimsical melds with harmony.
As twilight softens, joy climbs high,
Under the spell of a moonlit sky.

Enigma of the Climbing Shadows

In the yard, a plant took flight,
In the moon's glow, oh what a sight!
It climbed the fence with girlish glee,
As if to say, "Come dance with me!"

With every twist, it played a prank,
A leafy version of a prankster's flank.
It wrapped around my sleepy hat,
I chased it down, like a goofy cat!

The neighbors laughed, they couldn't sleep,
As I wrestled with the leafy creep.
In the end, we shared a hug,
The night ended, all snug as a bug!

So if you find your plants are bold,
Just know they crave some tales retold.
Not just in dreams, but reality too,
These climbing shadows are quite the crew!

Journey through an Emerald Labyrinth

I wandered through leaves, a maze so bright,
Each corner turned, a thrilling fright.
A pet spider waved, a friendly mate,
I yelled, "No, thanks! I'm on a date!"

Glorious greens, like a salad bowl,
The paths were wild, out of control.
I tripped on roots, and fell with grace,
A patch of mud became my embrace!

Birds overhead burst into song,
They cheered me on, right or wrong.
"You're the king of flops!" they'd scream and caw,
I grinned and took a clumsy bow!

But what delights this night imparts!
Messy fun fills giggling hearts.
So take a step, get lost, be free,
In the emerald maze, just be silly me!

Whispers of Twining Shadows

At dusk, whispers swept the ground,
A shadow dance, without a sound.
They curled and waved, a lively throng,
I couldn't help but hum along!

They told me tales of a wooden chair,
Whose legs got tangled, beyond repair.
"Just sit right here, we'll have some fun!"
But I toppled over—oh what a run!

A leafy hand gave me a lift,
Picking me up, it felt like a gift.
We floated past the fence so wide,
With shadows giggling by my side.

So when the darkness clings too tight,
Just join the whispers, dance with delight.
For in every twist and playful shove,
The shadows wink, in a playful love!

Entangled Fantasies of the Night

In the stillness, a tangle grew,
Like noodles spun, from me to you.
I tried to dance, but tied my shoe,
And down I went! Was this déjà vu?

A banana peel? Oh what a sight!
Entangled slowly, I took flight.
With every step, the world would spin,
"Hey buddy, try again!" they'd grin.

The humor set in; I roared with cheer,
As the shadows clapped and drew near.
They wrapped my feet in wild embrace,
A dance party now, at a snail's pace!

So if you find your dreams entwined,
Remember the laughs, the fun designed.
For tangled nights can be a treat,
Just laugh it off and dance your beat!

The Embrace of Hidden Pathways

In the garden where gnomes play,
I stumbled on a twisty way.
With socks that match my neighbor's cat,
I danced like a confused diplomat.

Behind the bushes, laughter swells,
As squirrels tell their nutty tales.
Chasing shadows, I lose my hat,
A combatant in this leafy sprawl spat!

A hedgehog joins, a little sly,
He rolls around, oh my, oh my!
Together we scheme, a punchline so neat,
The bushes erupt with our feel-good beat.

With nature's confetti in my hair,
I've found more friends here everywhere.
As evening's glow begins to gleam,
I sneak off, giggling, from this wild dream.

A Tapestry of Earthly Myths

With vines that giggle, roots that sing,
I met a frog wearing a crown—what a thing!
He croaked the tales of days gone by,
With every jump, he'd reach the sky.

A rabbit danced in polka spots,
While wiggling worms made funny thoughts.
They threw a party beneath the sun,
With carrot cake and sprightly fun!

The trees, they swayed, like folks on a spree,
Joined hands with shadows, sipping honey tea.
In this mythical realm of sheer delight,
The critters whispered, "Stay, don't fight!"

So I joined the feast, quite out of place,
With ants in tuxedos, a winning grace.
As laughter echoed, the sun tucked in,
I thanked the spirits for each silly sin.

Dreams Drifting on Leafy Currents

Floating along on feathered waves,
Among the leaves, my laughter braves.
A caper with squirrels, we share a jest,
In this dreamland, I'm truly blessed.

A dragonfly spins tales of woe,
While grasshoppers shout, "Give it a go!"
Each twist and turn brings a new surprise,
Moonlit giggles light up our eyes.

The flowers giggle, they dance like mad,
"Join our party, you silly lad!"
I twirl and whirl without any care,
Like a fool in love with the cool night air.

As shadows chuckle and starlight glows,
My leafy friends wear flowered bows.
In this world where whims abound,
I escape the mundane, joyfully unbound.

Nightshade's Gentle Caress

Beneath the cloak of midnight's sigh,
The groundlings plot and trick the sky.
With whispers sweet, they scheme and tease,
As fireflies gleam in joyful ease.

The owl wears spectacles, wise and keen,
He reads the scripts of the unseen.
While raccoons raid, they knock at fate,
With snacks and laughs—they can't be late!

A cat in a hat joins the parade,
She purrs and taps, not afraid to jade.
As shadows stretch and sprightly dance,
Together we swap a silly romance.

So grab your quirks and hold them tight,
For after the laughter, the dawn takes flight.
In nightshade's arms, we find a jest,
Where fun and shadows blend the best.

Shadows in the Emerald Sphere

In the garden, hats on heads,
Racing whispers, silly threads,
Rabbits taunt with hops so grand,
Chasing shadows, hand in hand.

Bumblebees wear sneakers bright,
Buzzing tunes in morning light,
Dancing leaves keep time with flair,
Swaying without a single care.

Giggling flowers, sprightly cheer,
Tickling toes as I draw near,
Petals laugh, a fickle jest,
Who knew flora could be the best?

A tangled mess of playful glee,
With leafy friends, I'm wild and free,
In this sphere of emerald hue,
I find the fun in all I do.

The Quiet Embrace of Flora

Beneath the ferns, I find my peace,
Where mushrooms talk and troubles cease,
Whispers echo, quiet charm,
Flora giggles, blooms disarm.

With leafy pals, we share tall tales,
Of tiny boats and beetle sails,
Sunlight winks from leafy nooks,
As critters plot in secret books.

I trip on roots, a clumsy dance,
The daisies giggle at my chance,
A snort from grass brings forth a cheer,
In nature's arms, I'll lose my fear.

The wildflowers draw a jolly scene,
Where daisies and dandelions convene,
In this embrace of green so silly,
Each shy plant just wants to be frilly.

Luminescent Threads of Memory

In twilight's glow, the jests unfold,
Nights forgotten, tales retold,
Fireflies wear their shining hats,
While crickets sing like chittering cats.

Each flicker tells a funny bit,
Of sneaky frogs and their big wit,
A tangle of laughter in the air,
With every giggle, light fills the square.

A slumbering snail dreams of a race,
Dared to challenge a turtle's pace,
With echoes of joy, we're never bland,
In this memory where fun expands.

The stars above keep watching near,
As we spin stories bright and clear,
Wrapped in laughter glowing bright,
In every thread, we find delight.

A Canopy of Unspoken Dreams

Under branches with silly hoots,
The giggling leaves wear tiny boots,
Squirrels chatter about their schemes,
Beneath this stretch of leafy dreams.

A jolly berry rolls away,
Whispering jokes to make me sway,
Mossy carpets, soft and green,
I tumble down, but I'm still keen.

The canopy drapes like a quilt,
Where joyous whispers are gently spilt,
Each branch a friend with stories anew,
As I weave through laughter, just me and you.

In this shade, I try to scheme,
To capture all my closest dreams,
But who knew that branches were so wise?
They laugh at me and say, "Surprise!"

Climbing Through Night's Embrace

In shadows thick, I trip and fall,
With leafy greens that tease my call.
A laughter blooms beneath the stars,
As I dodge branches of imaginary cars.

I climb a wall made of sour cream,
With dreams of pasta, it seems extreme.
The night giggles in tangled strands,
While I dance awkwardly, no one understands.

I leap through petals, scatter my fears,
Bouncing off moonlight, laughing cheers.
Twirls in the dark with a spaghetti crown,
Who knew the night could wear such a gown?

So here I am, in this tangled quest,
Chasing shadows, I must confess.
Each vine I meet, a snicker they bring,
In night's embrace, I remain the king!

The Lattice of Our Reveries

In a garden of giggles, plants sway and twirl,
Where carrots wear hats and the potatoes girl.
Jokes sprout freely on each leafy vine,
As laughter takes root, and we sip dandelion wine.

Through trellises woven with silly dreams,
The squash sings softly, or so it seems.
Tomatoes with glasses, critique the tunes,
While cucumbers boogie 'neath the laughing moons.

I dance with parsley, we waltz side by side,
With topsy-turvy jokes we cannot hide.
Each leafy embrace, a tickle of cheer,
In this lattice of mirth, there's nothing to fear.

So come join the folly in our greenened spree,
Where dreaming is fun and laughter is free.
In zany gardens, let's create some more,
With our twirling tales, who could ask for more?

Green Tendrils of Sorrow

Once I tripped over a leafy snare,
With tendrils grasping, it just seemed unfair.
The greens whispered stories, of mishaps so grand,
Like slipping on marbles in a parsnip band.

Pity me not, for I danced through the gloom,
With broccoli trees filling up every room.
In tears of laughter, we planted our seeds,
While broccoli crowns sprouted whimsical deeds.

Through moments of woe, I chuckled with glee,
A sprout of a joke, as funny as can be.
In gardens of chaos, we're never alone,
For every green sorrow has humor its own.

So raise up a toast to the tangled and wild,
Even sadness can wear a mischievous smile.
As we laugh through the night, let worries unfurl,
With green tendrils about, I'll enjoy this mad whirl!

Secrets Woven in the Moonlight

In moonbeam threads, secrets take flight,
As veggies gossip in the soft, silvery light.
Cucumbers whisper, 'Did you hear the news?'
While peas plan a party, in brightly colored shoes.

Under this cover, mischief is spun,
Carrot capers, oh what fun!
With leafy conspirators joined in a trance,
The garden's alive with a giggly dance.

The night plays tricks with its twinkling eyes,
A kaleidoscope of laughter under the skies.
In every nook, there's a chuckle or two,
As asparagus claps for the joy that ensues.

So let's twine our secrets, let's weave them anew,
With humor a-plenty and laughter that grew.
In moonlit mirth, let's paint the night bright,
With secrets and giggles, we'll share our delight!

Climbing Towards the Unknown

In my garden, quite absurd,
A beanstalk sprouted, so we heard.
It reached the clouds, then turned to dance,
Whispering jokes, it took a chance.

With every twist, it wore a hat,
Said, 'I'm not leafy, just a brat!'
Twirled around my neighbor's cat,
A comical sight; oh, imagine that!

It climbed to heights where dreams collide,
Chasing squirrels on a thrilling ride.
All were giggling, full of cheer,
As silly antics drew us near.

So up we went, not taking heed,
Of all the oddities we'd see.
With laughter trailing through the night,
We soared through wackiness—what a flight!

The Labyrinth of Leafy Whispers

In a maze where greens conspire,
A lettuce leaf sparks clever fire.
It chuckles at my clueless face,
While vines insist I lose my place.

Tomatoes wink, as if they know,
The way to tickle and to sow.
Cucumbers tease with slippery charm,
This verdant joke is such a balm.

With every twist, a new surprise,
The carrots laugh, in bright disguise.
A bean sprouts jokes, oh what a show,
In leafy dreams, the fun will grow!

So giggle here, and laugh some more,
In this garden maze, we will explore.
From leafy whispers, life unfurls,
In nature's jest, we twirl and twirl!

Flora's Dreamscape

In Flora's realm of leafy cheer,
Behind each petal hides a sneer.
The daisies wink, the roses grin,
As butterflies play hide-and-seek within.

A sunflower shouts, 'I'm tall, you know!'
With petals spread, it steals the show.
While daffodils chuckle, in a row,
At bees who dance, quite slow and low.

The nightshade giggles, but shh—it's shy,
While morning glories watch from high.
Each bloom holds secrets, wild and free,
In Flora's world, we all agree!

Who knew that petals could hold sway?
In dreams of green, we laugh and play.
So twirl and leap, let's take a chance,
In Flora's dreamscape, let's all dance!

Where the Wild Things Whisper

In hidden corners of the wood,
Where wild things play, we laugh for good.
A raccoon jests with cheeky flair,
While owls hoot secrets in the air.

The ferns spread whispers, quick and sly,
Telling tales as birds fly high.
The mushrooms giggle, round and stout,
Promising a crazy route!

With tangled roots and playful fun,
The critters scamper; oh, what a run!
In shadows cast where mischief starts,
We find surprise with all our hearts.

So join the dance, come wild and free,
In laughter's realm among the trees.
Where wild things whisper; let's dive deep,
And lose ourselves in giggles and sleep!

The Enigma of Knotted Paths

In the garden of thoughts, they twist and twine,
Rolling like laughter, they dance in a line.
Whispers of secrets in spirals they keep,
A puzzle of greens, where I stumble and leap.

A tangle of giggles arrives on the scene,
Nature's own puzzle, a green-joke machine.
With every wrong turn, I trip on a joke,
While tangled in roots, I embrace the folk.

Serenity in Twisting Blooms

A flowered riddle in petals and hue,
Bouncing with joy, as they dance in the dew.
They curl like pretzels, they spiral and sway,
Catching their giggles, they play and they play.

Oh, what a sight, those jests in the light,
A merry parade, such a charming delight.
I chuckle and ponder, where will they go?
Their antics are wild, like a circus in flow.

The Language of Unseen Trellises

In whispers of green, they chatter and boast,
Twisting through laughter, a playful host.
They speak in the rustle, a giggle and sigh,
A language of fun that floats up to the sky.

Dodging the thorns, they tease every step,
Like jesters in foliage, they sparkle and prep.
Each vine tells a tale, a story so bright,
A comedy act under the moon's silver light.

A Dream Weaver in Blossom's Shade

Under the blossom, a mischief brews,
Frolicking shadows with colorful views.
They tangle and giggle, a whimsical crew,
In the soft summer air, pulled into the blue.

With whispers of cheer, they spin and incite,
A festival of chuckles, oh what a sight!
I slide through their folly, a smile on my face,
In the shade of their laughter, I find my own place.

www.ingramcontent.com/pod-product-compliance
Lightning Source LLC
Chambersburg PA
CBHW070305120526
44590CB00017B/2570